ARP AND CIVIL
IN THE
SECOND WORLD WAR

Peter Doyle

SHIRE PUBLICATIONS

Published by Shire Publications Ltd,
PO Box 883, Oxford, OX1 9PL, UK
PO Box 3985, New York, NY 10185-3985, USA
Email: shire@shirebooks.co.uk   www.shirebooks.co.uk

First published 2010.
Transferred to digital print on demand 2014.

A CIP catalogue record for this book is available from the
British Library.

Shire Library no. 581   •   ISBN-13: 978 0 74780 765 0

Peter Doyle has asserted his right under the Copyright,
Designs and Patents Act, 1988, to be identified as the
author of this book.

Designed by Ken Vail Graphic Design, Cambridge, UK
Typeset in Perpetua and Gill Sans.
Printed and bound by PrintOnDemand-Worldwide.com,
Peterborough, UK

COVER IMAGE
NFS personnel in action at the site of a V1 flying bomb
attack in Upper Norwood, South London, on 1 July
1944. (IWM D 21248)

TITLE PAGE IMAGE
The Sterling Silver 'badge of appointment' worn by all
members of the ARP Services, designed by Eric Gill in
1937. Over 800,000 would be issued by 1939.

CONTENTS PAGE IMAGE
London communal shelter sign. Signs like this were
set up, dimly lit, in the blackout, directing people to
the shelter. No deep shelters were dug until late in the
war as official policy; instead, surface shelters were
built and garden 'Anderson' shelters distributed.

ACKNOWLEDGEMENTS
I would like to thank my friend and fellow author Paul
Evans for his support, and loan of his ARP poster. I am
grateful to the Trustees of the Imperial War Museum for
allowing the reproduction of images on pages 4, 11, 12,
13, 14, 16, 20, 24, 28, 31, 35, 36, 41, 46, 50, 52, and 58.
I would also like to thank Bella Bennett; Roy Goodey of
the London at War Study Group; Esther Mann, Lucy Price
and David Glennie of the London Fire Brigade Museum;
Chris Mees; Tim Richardson; Bob Seaton; Libby Simpson;
Stephen Wheeler, and many other people who have
supplied material and advice. Finally, I could not have
completed this work without the considerable support
of Julie and James.

IMPERIAL WAR MUSEUM COLLECTIONS
Some of the photos in this book come from the Imperial
War Museum's huge collections, which cover all aspects of
conflict involving Britain and the Commonwealth since the
start of the twentieth century. These rich resources are
available online to search, browse and buy at
www.iwmcollections.org.uk. In addition to Collections
Online, you can visit the Visitor Rooms, where you can
explore over 8 million photographs, thousands of hours of
moving images, the largest sound archive of its kind in the
world, thousands of diaries and letters written by people
in wartime, and a huge reference library. To make an
appointment, call (020) 7416 5320,
or e-mail mail@iwm.org.uk

Imperial War Museum www.iwm.org.uk

CONTENTS

BRITAIN IN THE FRONT LINE

DURING 1939–45, the British public were to experience warfare on an unprecedented scale, with every man, woman and child playing their part. While the armed services saw action across the globe, British citizens defended their home and homeland from aerial attack with resistance and fortitude on a scale never before seen. Carrying out this vital work was a well-equipped, well-trained and well-motivated 'army' of civilians, whose sole purpose was to prevent loss of life and property from the attentions of 'Firebomb Fritz' (as the posters dubbed their enemy). The purpose of this book is to explain the actions of these unarmed civil defence workers in the six years of the Second World War. In so doing, it might provide a brief introduction for family historians and others wishing to know what it was like to be, for example, an air raid warden in Glasgow or an auxiliary fireman during the London Blitz. Although it cannot hope to be comprehensive, this book will give some sense of the roles of Britain's home defenders during the conflict.

Although the beginnings of war sprang on the scene dramatically in 1939, most people were already resigned to the fact that it was a very definite possibility. Since at least 1935, people in Britain had been watching conflicts begin in Africa and Spain, and had observed the growing threat from Hitler's resurgent and aggressive regime across the English Channel. With the rise of Hitler came the death knell for the Versailles Treaty (and with it the largely passive approach of the League of Nations) that had settled the First World War and had left Germany with huge war debts. Hitler's approach in the reconstruction of his new Germany was undeniably belligerent. His armed forces – supposedly restricted by the terms of Versailles – were built up, and a new air force constructed around its supposedly civilian core. With his resentment of the terms of the treaty came the possibility that Hitler would target his nation's old adversaries. The possibility of an aerial assault on Britain, so close to continental Europe, had to be entertained. War was in the air, and what had previously seemed a remote possibility – the use of poison gas, and the concentrated use of high explosives against civilians – had become a reality in the conflicts in Abyssinia and Spain in 1936.

Opposite:
The Blitz: Ludgate Circus in the City of London, 11 May 1940.
(IWM HU36221)

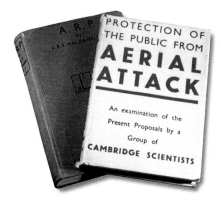

PROTECTION OF THE PUBLIC FROM AERIAL ATTACK

An examination of the Present Proposals by a Group of
CAMBRIDGE SCIENTISTS

Intellectuals predicted the mass destruction of British cities by aerial bombardment – this was to influence the pacifist movements of the 1930s.

ARP – Air Raid Precautions – became a well-known acronym in the prelude to war. Postcards like this were one way of getting used to it.

Within the climate of fear existing in the 1930s, scholars and politicians had been predicting what would happen if another world war were to break out. They concluded that vast aerial armadas would destroy cities with high explosives, and target the civilian populations with gas. Clearly apparent to everyone was that, with advances in aircraft design, Britain was no longer secure in its island home; this had already been proven in the First World War, when Zeppelin and bomber raids had terrorised London and the south-east of England. The primitive home defences of 1914–18 had been clearly inadequate; so if war was inevitable, then Britain should be ready.

As a result, in 1924 the Committee of Imperial Defence, charged with the defence of the United Kingdom, set up a subcommittee to consider issues of the protection of the United Kingdom from aerial attack. Then called 'Air Raid Precautions' or 'ARP', it was formed under the leadership of a senior civil servant, Sir John Anderson, the Lord Privy Seal. For a decade this subcommittee was to consider a host of issues arising from the experience of the Great War and the development of new aerial weapons; issues that would materially affect the defence of the civilian population from aerial attack. Discussions ranged over whether shelters should be constructed, gas masks issued, vulnerable citizens evacuated and lighting restrictions introduced. These deliberations – all of which were to be implemented in war – were carried out confidentially, and were to influence the British approach to what was then termed 'passive air defence'.

In mainland Europe, Hitler's rise to power in the wake of the failures of the Weimar Republic was to quicken the defence plans and cement them in the UK. As such, born out of Sir John Anderson's committee was the more tangible Air Raid Precautions (ARP) Department, created at the Home Office in direct response to the rearmament of Germany, and Hitler's growing and blatant ambitions. From 1 April 1935, the ARP Department was to direct the development of passive air defence in Britain, in response to the growing threat. On 1 January 1938, the new Air Raid Precautions Act came into force, compelling local authorities to take

A. R. P.
all - Right - Presently
THE SNUGGERY
WHEN THE WARNING SIRENS GO
WE'LL DO THE LAMBETH WALK BELO'
NO NEED TO PUSH OR MAKE A
SO DOWN THE HOLE WITH '
THAT'S

A. R. P.
all - Right - Presently
THE CUBBY 'OLE
TAKE IT EASY –
NO HELTER-SKELTER
TO THE BETTER 'OLE
THE AIR RAID SHELTER;
NEVER GET WHITE
AROUND THE GILLS
WE'RE SAFE AS THE BANK
FROM HITLER'S PILLS!

action to set up and train their ARP services. The ARP Act also brought with it the intent to expand the police and the fire services – always considered the front line of civil defence, as they had been in the First World War. Volunteers would be needed to fight the flames and keep order; the Auxiliary Fire Service (AFS) and Police Reserves were other options for the volunteer. The new services, a largely volunteer civilian 'army', began recruitment in earnest in 1937.

In Europe, Hitler's territorial ambitions were focused, initially at least,

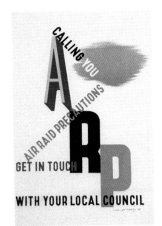

Left: Recruitment to the ARP Services was slow prior to the Munich Crisis of September 1938, but posters like this helped swell the ranks.

Below: A set of cigarette cards was issued by Players, which acted as a guide to dealing with ARP matters: gas, incendiaries and casualties.

on uniting the German-speaking peoples in Germany and Austria, and creating a new European order with the Third Reich at its centre. In Hitler's vision, the new Reich would need room for expansion, and the German Chancellor set his sights first on neighbouring Czechoslovakia, with its partly ethnic-German population. Nervously, Prime Minister Chamberlain sought to buy time for a Britain whose armed forces were severely under-resourced through years of post-war neglect. The possibility of the doomed Munich Conference of September 1938 removing the threat of war with Nazi Germany was remote, and, as Chamberlain negotiated away the Sudetenland and Hitler's troops marched into Czechoslovakia, the preparations for the 'passive defence' of Britain were quickened. During an intense period of doubt and concern, the British Government and its Chiefs of Staff raced to prepare the country, rearming and re-equipping its forces, and enacting the planned ARP preparations. Though voluntary, ARP recruitment was low in the early days; this was to change after Munich, and with the ARP-coordinated issue of civilian gas masks, ARP wardens were much in demand and much in evidence.

Initial reactions to the new ARP Service were at best lukewarm, and at worst hostile, especially to the 400,000 or so full-time paid personnel (a figure to be slashed by half during the 'Phoney War' period due to public pressure). An atmosphere of inevitable war brought with it a rash of texts advising on the construction of air-raid shelters, and on the preparation of gas-proof refuge rooms. In an act of final preparation on the eve of war, Sir John Anderson issued leaflets from his department at the Home Office that urged civilians to ready themselves for the coming conflict. For them, there would be no deep underground shelters. Instead, shelter trenches were dug, and communal surface shelters were constructed with concrete roofs – widely held to be death traps. It was hardly surprising that Londoners would flock to the security of the Underground, despite official resistance. That resistance would fold with the coming of the Blitz, and Tube shelterers would be regularised. For most others, sheltering at home – either in 'Anderson' shelters dug into the garden, or in unwieldy steel 'table' or 'Morrison' shelters – was the best, if not only, option.

The ARP Services were there to help deliver the Government's official policy of readying the population for war, and to engage the public in making plans for their own personal protection. In 1938, it was decided that gas

Crypts, basements and other secure facilities were designated as ARP shelters; signs like this one indicated how many people they could safely hold.

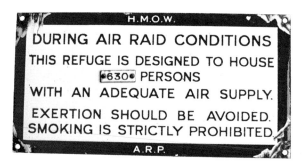

H.M.O.W.

DURING AIR RAID CONDITIONS
THIS REFUGE IS DESIGNED TO HOUSE
●630● PERSONS
WITH AN ADEQUATE AIR SUPPLY.
EXERTION SHOULD BE AVOIDED.
SMOKING IS STRICTLY PROHIBITED.
A.R.P.

masks would be issued to all who would need one – effectively the whole population of 40 million, at a projected cost of £5.5 million – and these masks were to be issued, fitted and checked by the men and women of the ARP. At first, these respirators were issued only to adults and older children – the cause of much understandable alarm – but smaller children and babies were to receive their own in good time. Plans were also drawn up for the large-scale evacuation of children, expectant mothers and the frail from the heart of Britain's cities. This was where the attacks would come, and those most vulnerable would need to be moved for their own safety.

After declaration of war on 3 September 1939, the anticipated aerial onslaught failed to materialise. Although there were a few early false alarms, the 'Phoney War' period was a tough one for the recently mobilised volunteers of the ARP, the Auxiliary Fire Service, and the Police War Reserves. Labelled the 'Darts Brigade' by some (implying a leisurely existence of darts matches, dominoes and cards), these volunteers had to suffer a long period of inactivity, from the outbreak of war until the first real bombing of Britain, with the result that morale and the confidence of the people were shaken. This was dispelled when the first bombs landed in Britain, the very first being in Hoy, Orkney, on 17 October 1939. The first civilian killed by bombing was also in Orkney, six months after the outbreak of war, on 16 March 1940. Bombing of mainland Britain – in Kent and north-east England – came in May, with the first daylight attacks in July.

Below left: The Civilian gas mask – some six million were distributed, with special versions for young children (and a hood for babies), asthmatics and other people with breathing difficulties and facial deformities.

Below: Wardens would ensure that the mask fitted properly; contaminated air was taken in through the filter, and exhaled breath released from the sides of the mask. Placing a card over the filter tested the efficiency and fit of the mask. (IWM D3912)

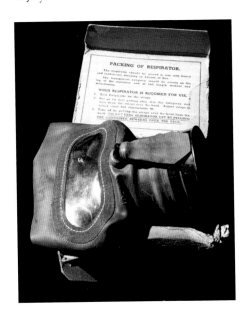

The Heinkel He 111 bomber (pictured prior to the London Blitz, in the *Illustrated London News* for 21 July 1940), one of the mainstays of the *Luftwaffe* bomber fleet, and no stranger to British airspace. With two engines, a relatively small bomb-bay, and under-armed, it was vulnerable to fighter attack. After the first daylight raids, Göring was forced to switch his tactics to night attack.

The opening of the Battle of Britain in early August saw major ports and airfields targeted and heavily bombed. London was to receive its first raid on 24 August, when an off-course flight of Heinkel He 111 bombers released its load over the city – a load intended for aircraft factories and oil refineries in Kent. The RAF was to retaliate, and Berlin was bombed on 25 August, a city previously considered untouchable by the Nazis. From then on, the pace of raids against civilian targets quickened. Fatefully, on Saturday 7 September – the beginning of the 'London Blitz' proper – Reichsmarschall Herman Göring despatched his bombers en masse to batter down London and the

Göring moves his attention to London; the first day of the London Blitz, 7 September 1940. During the attack, fierce fires rage in the dock area behind Tower Bridge. (IWM NYT4735F)

will of its people. Flying in daylight, but bombing until the early morning, 375 or so bombers with fighter support attacked targets across the East End of London and its docks, the City, and as far west as Kensington and Westminster. This was the only major daylight raid over the capital; at 8 o'clock that evening a new raid commenced, a raid that once more wrought havoc across the City and the East End. The death toll was 450; 1,600 people were injured and thousands of homes were damaged. The ARP Services were fully committed. Fires raged across the bombed areas – the wharves and storehouses packed with a diversity of materials from grain to rum created problems rarely seen by the London Fire Brigade, never mind the unblooded Auxiliary Fire Service. Göring's strategic gamble meant that the Luftwaffe was now committed to the bombing of London and other major cities and conurbations within the United Kingdom. Attention was turned from Operation *Seelöwe* (Sealion) – the proposed invasion of Britain – and the affair was shelved forever after 15 September, Battle of Britain Day, the heaviest raid, during which it became apparent that the RAF was unbeaten.

For every night in September, between 50 and 300 bombers attacked London. In that month alone, 10,000 bombs were dropped over London; 5,750 people were killed, with 10,000 more injured. The attacks continued well into October – 57 nights without break, in which

War damage is still apparent in London. The Guards' Memorial opposite Horse Guards Parade still carries the scars of the Blitz today.

Right:
The Underground
'Tube' system was
favoured by
Londoners seeking
shelter from the
Blitz. Not officially
sanctioned until
late in 1940, the
Tube shelters
eventually became
regularised. This is
Elephant and
Castle, in the heart
of blitzed London,
on 11 November
1940.
(IWM D 1568)

Below: A shelter
ticket for Elephant
and Castle Tube
station, issued to
a local housewife.
Regular Tube
shelterers had to
apply for such
tickets; others
could queue for
tickets on a nightly
basis.

the air raid sirens were heard across the capital, and during which the people of London would seek refuge in the shelter of the Tube. Thousands of homes and businesses were damaged and destroyed. The infrastructure of the capital was severely affected: railways, electricity supply, water, gas. Fires burned in major conflagrations that destroyed the heart of the capital – miraculously sparing St Paul's Cathedral – most intense during the fire-raids of 29 December 1940 (the 'Second Great Fire of London') and 10 May 1941. In this three-month period of the Blitz on London alone, 12,696 people were killed, and an

Latham Street in Poplar, in the East End of London, destroyed by a land mine – marine mines redeployed to devastating effect against land targets. Here a wrecked Anderson shelter has saved the lives of its three shelterers. (IWM D 5949)

The cover of the *Illustrated London News* for 21 September 1940, with a famous Cecil Beaton image used to dramatic effect in condemning the barbarism of the bombing of civilian targets.

additional 20,000 people injured. The lives of many more families would be permanently blighted in this way before the war was to end.

By the end of the intense Blitz on London in July 1941, it is thought that something like 45–50,000 individual high explosive bombs fell on the city, amounting to 7,500 tons, a figure dwarfed by the great mass of incendiaries intended to create fires that would rage out of control in densely packed streets. This intensity of bombing was endured not only by London, but also Coventry, Birmingham, Merseyside, Manchester, Clydeside, Portsmouth, Plymouth and many other industrial towns and port cities across the nation in the early years of the war. These and other centres would be targeted by bombers carrying HE bombs of all sizes, sea mines redeployed as land mines, and incendiary bombs ranging from the 1 kg Electron to the much larger oil bomb. In all, 51,500 civilians were killed.

The Allied bombing of German cities – particularly the medieval jewel of Lübeck – brought retribution against historic targets in Britain. The Baedeker raids (so-called as the targets were seemingly chosen from the famous

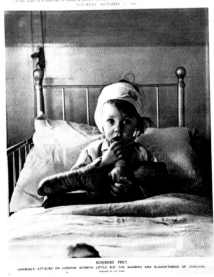

THE ILLUSTRATED LONDON NEWS

13

A V1 flying bomb hits its target at Aldwych, near Drury Lane in the West End of London, 30 June 1944. (IWM HU 638)

National Air Raid Distress Fund charity flags. With so many people homeless, there was great need for assistance.

guide books) of mid-1942 saw the bombing of Bath, Canterbury, Exeter, Norwich and York, with the loss of several architectural gems, and 1,600 lives. London would be bombed again in January 1944, when over 400 aircraft were launched from French airfields against the capital in the 'Little Blitz'. Largely ineffective, this interval of bombing was superseded by the use of the pilotless 'V-weapons' offensive.

On 12 June 1944, the first V1 was launched at London, with over 9,250 sent across the Channel. Popularly known as the 'doodlebug' or 'buzz bomb', it would be observed in flight, falling once the engine had cut out to deliver its payload. Fortunately, a large proportion was destroyed in flight, but 2,515 reached London, killing 6,184 civilians and injuring 17,981. More terrifying were the V2 rockets, first used against London in September. Around 1,115 were fired at Britain from launch sites in the Low Countries, killing around 2,750 people. Unlike the V1 weapons, there was little that could be done against V2s, and most found a target, though many fell short in the fields of Kent.

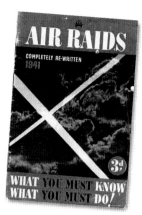

Air Raids, What You Must Know. What You Must Do! A Ministry of Home Security pamphlet of 1941.

The Blitz of 1940–1 saw Britain battered but undefeated. Respite came only when Hitler turned his attention eastwards, his bombers redeployed against the Soviet Union, his attention turned away from the destruction of the British will and resolve. London was not the only city to suffer. From then on the services of all the major towns and cities throughout the United Kingdom would be severely stretched, with many suffering their own intense period of blitz. Through it all, the Civil Defence services were undaunted. Their training and resolve had been tested to the limit in some cases. The planning for ARP had proved its worth. Wardens became respected and trusted members of a highly motivated force that included men and women dedicated to supporting the average householder. Once-amateur firefighters of the AFS could now stand proudly shoulder-to-shoulder with the professional firemen of the pre-war service. Many had been killed, but the services held, the towns and cities returned to normal. Would they have been overwhelmed if Britain had been visited by the intensity of attacks brought against Germany in 1944–5? In the post-war opinion of Sir Aylmer Firebrace, Chief of the Fire Staff, perhaps, but the fact is that with each new twist in the aerial assault brought against Britain, the men and women of the Civil Defence Services were able to meet the threat head on.

At their peak in 1942, the Civil Defence and Fire Services numbered one and a quarter million men and women. In the words of the official historian: 'Although the threat of German air bombardment [of Britain] varied in intensity, it would be wrong not to regard it as continuous ... the civil defence organisation had to remain alert and manned throughout the five and a half years of war.' This is their story.

London was not the only target. After the sustained 'May Blitz' on Birkenhead and Liverpool in 1941, two wardens assist an injured woman from an ARP Post. (IWM HU 36162)

THE ARP SERVICES

THE CENTRAL PLANK of Britain's approach to civil defence was the development of its ARP Services. ARP – Air Raid Precautions – was an acronym much used in the prelude to war; the term summarised the passive nature of the protection to be provided. With air raids expected to be a terrifying aspect of new conflict, so precautions should be put in place to deal with the consequences of the raiders getting through. There was nothing the ARP could do to prevent the bombing of the nation's cities, but there was plenty to do to help protect lives and livelihoods once the bombs inevitably fell.

The Government's approach to ARP was regional, based on twelve civil defence regions, and inherently local, with wardens providing the link between the public and the Government. On the advent of war, the overall direction for ARP Services passed to a new ministry – the Ministry of Home Security – which would administer its actions through a regional structure. There were ten regions in England (the most populous country), and one each for Scotland and Wales. Each region had a commissioner who was answerable to the Minister for Home Security (Sir John Anderson initially, then, from 1941, Herbert Morrison), but who would take charge of their regions as autocrats if the invader were to come.

The ARP Services provided men and women who were locally recruited, would have the confidence of the local population, and would be trained to deal with any emergency that the enemy could throw at them. As originally planned, the ARP Services were to include several specialist branches: Wardens, Rescue, Gas Decontamination, Ambulance and First Aid, all coordinated by a Report and Control Service, itself informed by Messengers. These services would be required to deal, on an intimate, street-by-street basis, with the citizens of Britain, guiding them, assisting them, and, when the time came, helping to rescue them from danger. The majority of ARP workers were part-timers, working a maximum of 48 hours a month, with full-time personnel paid at a rate of £3 a week (£2 a week for women) – earning them, and their fellow volunteers in the Auxiliary Fire Service,

Opposite: An ARP Warden, 1941. (IWM D 3980)

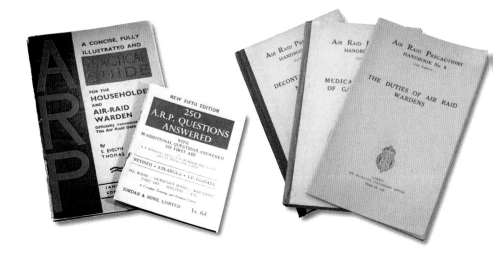

Above: ARP guides. Commercial publishers were quick to supply guide books for the education of budding ARP workers and the public alike.

Above right: A range of official handbooks was produced for ARP in the pre- and early-war period.

the undeserved name of 'three-quid-a-week army dodgers'. Such names fell away with the first fall of bombs on the towns and cities of Britain.

As set out in ARP Handbook No. 6, *Air Raid Precautions in Factories and Business Premises* (1936), most large commercial concerns had responsibility for their own ARP Services. These were to act as a back-up and supplement to the main ARP Services. The Civil Defence Act of 1939 had made it clear that larger manufacturing and commercial firms would have to train a percentage of staff to deal with ARP, to the tune of 10 per cent of the total establishment. By June 1940, there were at least 150,000 men and women engaged in such services. To mark and recognise their voluntary service, a bewildering array of buttonhole badges was produced, usually bearing the name of the firm, sometimes indicating the nature of the service.

The role of air raid warden was to be one of the most important in the prosecution of the Government's policy that civil defence basically began at home. In exhorting the public to construct refuge rooms, to take care of their gas masks, and to consider the protection of their families through the masking and blackout of windows, the local ARP warden was a key figure. ARP Handbook No. 8, *The Duties of Air Raid Wardens* (1938), gave clear indications on the type of character needed: 'the air raid warden is chosen as a responsible and reliable member of the public who will undertake to advise and help his fellow citizens, in the sector to which he is allotted, in all the risks and calamities which might follow from air attack, and will form a link between them and the authorities for reporting air raid damage and calling aid when required.'

An industrial ARP buttonhole badge. Each major industrial and commercial firm produced their own versions, now avidly collected.

The guide was at pains to point out that these duties would apply equally to men and women.

Wardens, then, were local, intimate with the neighbourhood, and knowledgeable about the streets and alleyways of their patch. Yet wardens still had to be easily identifiable to newcomers and out-of-towners; as such, a variety of signs and identifying marks were produced so that they could be contacted at home, and called out in an emergency. The Government hoped that, in time of crisis, friendly advice (and enforcement) from a local would help to steady the neighbourhood, and assist with a multitude of tasks from gas mask fitting, to the digging-in of Anderson shelters. Blackout enforcement was an early responsibility of the ARP. With no bar to age or gender, this individual was the Government's proxy, and the lifeline of support for the elderly, infirm, frightened or insecure. Roughly one in six wardens were women.

Locally known, locally based, it would be the warden's duty to ensure that all were accounted for, that incidents be logged, and if necessary, that the actions of other civil defence teams on the ground were coordinated when they were required. Wardens would be amongst the most important people on the ground during the Blitz. The operational unit was that of the Warden's Post, usually covering an area of up to a quarter of a mile square in a built-up area and encompassing roughly 500 people. Warden's Posts were conspicuous and signposted; during the Blitz, the visible presence of helmeted wardens greatly helped to calm the public.

The Warden's Post was one of the most important components in the organisation of civil defence. Located at street corners, suburban turnings and main roads, Warden's Posts provided important outposts from the local control centre, with the Post Warden supplying information to, and receiving instruction from, the local ARP Control Centre. From here, wardens could be dispatched to 'incidents' (as air raids were then called), and messengers sent to Control. Most posts were protected by some form of structure, often partly underground but equally as often built on the surface. Typical examples include brick-built versions roofed with a concrete slab. This type of construction was used widely for large civilian surface air-raid shelters, and was almost completely mistrusted by the public, who believed, with some

1st Warden:—"You'd better knock at the door."

2nd Warden:—"Blimey! Bill, what a pity!"

In the 'Phoney War' period, ARP wardens were objects of derision – particularly with their attention to the enforcement of the 'blackout'.

Cheerful and defiant, a white-helmeted Post Warden outside his post in Poplar, London.
(IWM D5943)

reason, that such shelters would collapse, the concrete roof crushing their occupants. Other local authorities used more concrete in construction, or even steel one- or two-person shelters that could be moved with an appropriate crane.

Each Warden's Post was well equipped to deal with emergencies. Anti-gas suits, gloves, boots, eye-shields and curtains were present, as were whistles, hand rattles and hand bells for alerting the public to gas and bomb attack, and sundry other equipment. Torches, first aid supplies (replenished from ARP Control), and stirrup pumps made up the remainder of the equipment, alongside an incident ledger, and a sheath of paperwork to be filled in by the Post Warden before, during, and after raids.

The whistle. ARP wardens were to sound this to reinforce the sound of the air-raid siren, and later on, to announce the fall of incendiary bombs.

On an individual basis, wardens were issued with equipment specified by the ARP Department. Local authorities issued a variety of 'Cards of Appointment' for members of their services; alongside their National Registration Identity Cards, and silver ARP badges, these provided proof of authority as well as identity. They were intended, in the words of the ARP handbook No. 8, *The Duties of Air Raid Wardens* (1938), 'to be something the warden can show as evidence of his position when he visits householders and others in the course of his duties'. Wardens would also be equipped with steel helmet and gas mask; this was to be added to with the first issues of uniform in the form of an overall or coat, and then finally, a more practical wool uniform. Whistles were an essential part of the equipment of the ARP warden. It was intended that whistles would be sounded as a reinforcement of the alarm given by the 'low warbling note' of the air-raid siren. Later, the whistle was used to indicate the presence of the incendiaries so commonly associated with the latter stages of the Blitz.

Card of Appointment, and silver ARP badge for a warden in St Albans.

The ARP Civilian Duty Respirator, more robust than the standard civilian gas mask; other members would be issued with the military issue Service Respirator.

The protection of the public from gas attack was, in pre-war planning at least, the number one priority of the ARP Services. ARP wardens were responsible for issuing gas masks to the public, and checking them regularly to see that they were functioning. People were advised to carry their gas masks at all times, but lost property offices soon filled up with lost and discarded masks. The flimsy nature of the civilian mask, constructed from thin sheet rubber, a rubber band and a tinned filter, was not thought to be adequate to stand up to the rigours of service in the ARP. As such, the Chemical Defence Establishment at Porton Down designed a mask for the ARP Services, known as the Duty Respirator, with a more substantial moulded face piece, similar to that of the military issue mask.

At the first indication of gas attack, wardens were instructed to use gas rattles, first used alongside improvised gongs to warn of gas attack in the trenches

Right: ARP rattle and bell. The rattle was to be sounded to announce a gas attack; the bell was used to signify the all clear.

of the First World War. Rattles had the twin advantage that their sound was both distinctive and loud. They would be sounded by wardens; gas would be detected by sight, smell – wardens were trained to be alert to the smells of pear drops, horseradish and geraniums (indicating war gases such as KSK teargas, mustard gas and lewisite) – and by the gas-detector paint on the tops of pillar boxes, which changed colour in the presence of gas. War gas charts were regularly issued to update wardens and the public to the threats. To give the all clear, wardens would use hand bells. Both bells and rattles were essential items at the Warden's Post. In reality, there were no gas attacks on civilians during the Second World War, though the fear was very real.

Reporting, recording and logging 'incidents' were extremely important parts of an air raid warden's responsibilities, and all wardens got used to filling in the official forms. 'ARP/M1' forms were completed for each incident. In addition, information on all such incidents was logged in a ledger kept at each Warden's Post; this information was collated from all Posts, and plotted on

Below: ARP report (ARP/M1) and message (ARP/M3) forms.

a map and incident board at the Control Centre. Ultimately, this ensured that appropriate aid could be directed to the incident, the Control Centre coordinating Fire, Ambulance and Rescue parties on the advice of information received. Getting messages to the Control Centre was therefore of great importance; telephones were one way of dealing with the supply of information, but these were unreliable in wartime, and could be cut off. Messengers, carrying handwritten 'ARP/M3' forms were therefore invaluable. They were usually young people who acted as runners between Control Centres and Warden's Posts. Messengers were an essential part of the ARP set-up.

Left: ARP on the front cover of the popular weekly *Picture Post*. A man of the rescue service surveys the scene.

Below: Well-used early-war ARP 'bluette' overall uniform of a member of the Rescue Service, equipped with Civilian Duty Respirator, steel helmet, ARP axe, and incendiary bomb scoop.

The Rescue Service was trained in all aspects of the rescue of people from bombed houses; usually made up of skilled men, it was later to be divided into Heavy and Light Rescue branches. Rescue teams were highly trained in working through the ruins in search of survivors, in construction issues and shoring. Often requiring heavy equipment, each Rescue Party was equipped with a lorry packed with essential tools and equipment. These men understood the value in using their bare hands to dig out individuals, and exactly where to operate in both searching for survivors, and working through the ruins. Dogs would also be used. Where necessary, emergency shoring would be carried out to prevent buildings from collapsing, and it was often the case that rescue men, other members of the ARP, the AFS and the police would be engaged together on a major incident.

Given the Government's emphasis on the possibility of gas attack, the need to send out specialist Decontamination Squads to deal with everything from streets to individual properties was taken seriously. Such squads of seven

Decontamination squad in action during a pre-war exercise. (IWM D 3919)

individuals armed with lorries, protective clothing and bleaching powder were ready for action and were based at regularly spaced gas cleansing stations, usually maintained at council depots. The fear of poison gas attack, which derived from the experience of the First World War, resulted in a concentration of ARP literature and guidebooks on the subject of personal protection from gas. These commenced with the advice that individual homes should have a refuge room (echoed some decades later by the Cold War 'fall-out' room), with all cracks and holes stopped and basic sanitation laid on.

Following a gas attack, it was expected that whole areas would have to be decontaminated; fully equipped specialist decontamination units would operate from lorries, and would be called to the scene where needed. Gas Identification Officers were appointed from chemistry teachers and others with chemical skills; they would identify the threat, and were equipped with specialist field identification sets and badges bearing the initials 'GIO'. Decontamination was one of the essential ARP Services; its members were equipped with oilskin anti-gas suits, composed of separate jackets, trousers, gloves, overshoe coverings and hoods. Fortunately, such measures were never needed.

The ARP Control Centre was the nerve centre of local ARP (later Civil Defence) operations, sifting information on bombing 'incidents', keeping a situation map, and calling out services as required. Later, in 1941, 'Incident Officers', distinguished by their blue-covered steel helmets, coordinated actions on the ground. In all cases, messengers were vital in maintaining the communication links between the various services, especially when other means of communication failed; they were generally young men and women of pre-call-up age, from 16 onwards. First Aid Posts were a major part of the local ARP infrastructure, and were serviced by doctors, nurses and nursing auxiliaries. First Aid Parties (Stretcher Parties in London) also attended incidents, and the wounded were removed to safety by the Auxiliary Ambulance Service, using a variety of purloined cars for walking wounded, through to full ambulance transport for the more serious cases.

In keeping with the civilian basis of this 'force', no uniforms were issued to the early volunteers of the various ARP Services; instead, the hallmarked silver 'ARP' badge was to be worn. These badges were designed by typographer and sculptor Eric Gill, and were manufactured, initially at least, in hallmarked sterling silver by the Royal Mint. To qualify for the badge, a course of training had to be completed. By 1943, manufacture of the badge had completely stopped, with the more formal adoption of uniform and

Above: Shoulder flashes of some of the ARP branches, worn on the battledress uniform.

Left: ARP worker with buttonhole badge.

Below: Civil Defence armband, issued in response to calls for a uniform.

the change of emphasis in title away from 'ARP' to 'Civil Defence'. However, in response to the demands from ARP workers for a unique uniform, an official armband was sanctioned, finished in dark blue bearing the printed words 'Civil Defence' in 'old gold' in an arc, the new emblem of the service. Listening to pleas of the volunteers, from late 1939 the ARP Department started issuing a simple 'boiler suit'-type overall to all men, with a single-breasted coat version for women, and by 1941, a 'midnight' blue battledress was issued for the ARP, now fully retitled Civil Defence. With the issue of the Civil Defence battledress came the need for a series of identifying marks and badges, items that would identify clearly the rank and branch of service of the individual. The battledress blouse was issued with a simple circular cloth breast badge comprising the letters 'CD' in 'old gold' surmounted by a crown. Area markings – usually embroidered bars or arcs – were also worn beneath this badge.

Topping this off, and in common with all other Civil Defence services, the ARP wore the same steel helmet as issued to the military. No other headgear was issued to the ARP in the early stages of the war, and as such, when on parade, it was expected that the steel helmet would be worn. A beret would be issued later. In August 1939, it was agreed that helmets would be painted black for most members of the ARP Services, each branch distinguished by a two-inch-high

Civil Defence battledress uniform issued to supersede the early 'bluette' overalls, from a warden in the city of Salisbury, and equipped with steel helmet and Civilian Duty Respirator.

Two old soldiers, veterans of the Great War, in Civil Defence battledress, with badges of appointment.

white painted letter. In London, lettering was adopted both front and back of the helmet; elsewhere in the country, the most appropriate letter was applied only to the front. Typical examples are: W for Wardens; R for Rescue personnel; FAP for First Aid Parties (or, in London, the equivalent SP for Stretcher Parties); A for Ambulance; M for Messenger and DC for Decontamination Squads. Whereas most ARP workers had black helmets, a plain white helmet with black lettering was indicative of Rescue and Stretcher Party Leaders and Post Wardens.

London ARP warden's black helmet. London helmets were generally marked front and back with insignia.

Following early derision as part of the 'Darts Brigade', the ARP Services were to be tested during the Blitz of 1940, and from 1941 the term ARP would be superseded by the title 'Civil Defence'. The service had come of age.

White Post Warden helmets. White hats signified officers in the ARP.

THE AUXILIARY FIRE SERVICE (AFS)

THE AUXILIARY FIRE SERVICE, or AFS – 'heroes with grimy faces' as Winston Churchill was to call its members – is the subject of a great deal of interest. An organisation of volunteers liable for call-up to full-time paid service in time of war, the AFS attracted sufficient artists and authors to its rank and file to leave a rich legacy of literature and images which document the struggle against the flames – including the acclaimed documentary film *Fires Were Started*. Yet this legacy, and the raising of the National Fire Service in 1941, has meant that the role of the regular brigades in the 1940–1 Blitz has been overshadowed. In most cases, the AFS was to work alongside the brigade men who manned the red-painted pumps – thereby joining the 'red riders' of the London Fire Brigade (LFB). This was also true of countless other boroughs up and down the country.

The AFS was born of pre-war civil defence planning, when it was realised that the bombing of Britain's towns and cities in any future conflict would bring with it a great strain on the existing county fire brigades. Although high explosives and gas were considered the most damaging weapons to be used by the enemy in any future conflict, bombing would inevitably bring with it a need for fire control. From January 1938, the Government urged local authorities to consider the expansion of their fire services, including the recruitment of volunteers to a new volunteer service, the AFS. The Fire Brigades Act of July 1938 – allowing local authorities two years to expand their brigades – gave the green light to expansion, and a series of local campaigns was launched to bring men and women into the new service. Recruitment to the AFS, as with all the voluntary services prior to Munich, was slow, and much encouragement was needed. Posters and cinema slides were used to encourage volunteers to join. Information booklets were very necessary, persuading individuals of their role in the new service. By the end of 1938, only 80,000 volunteers had joined the service; but by the declaration of war the number had doubled to close to the required 200,000 auxiliary firefighters. Ultimately, the recruiting drives were successful, and by the end of 1941 the newly

Opposite:
A London
Auxiliary Fireman
operates a trailer
pump.
(IWM D 2611)

29

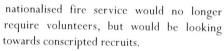

Above: A Norwich Auxiliary Fire Service crew (and immaculate regular) pose as 'red-riders', 1940.

Right: Recruitment pamphlet for the London Auxiliary Fire Service.

Women's Auxiliary Fire Service magazine for 1941.

nationalised fire service would no longer require volunteers, but would be looking towards conscripted recruits.

The Auxiliary Fire Service backed up the county and regional brigades from its inception. There were in fact two services, the AFS and the Women's AFS. The first of these, the firemen, were charged with dealing with the fires themselves; the second, a whole host of essential duties, including the efficient running of the emergency call centres, driving (including the taxis and other vehicles pressed into service to pull trailer pumps) and a range of ancillary services, including catering and welfare. In more than one case, firewomen were called upon to deal with fires on their own stations – situated in a wide range of locations to spread the possibility of knock-out – during raids, and many were decorated in the line of duty.

Firemen of the AFS qualified into the service after six months of training – this was reduced in June 1939 to within one month of joining. All trained volunteers to the AFS qualified for a lapel badge, which was worn with ordinary clothes to distinguish them. This badge was designed by the Royal Mint, with the AFS monogram in a red circle, surmounted by a crown, the same as that used in red letters on the AFS uniform jackets. This badge was worn high on the left side (between buttons two and three) of both the double-breasted wool fire tunic and overalls by the men of the AFS. The cap badge was simple: the AFS monogram set in a star, not surmounted by a crown, easily distinguishing it from the later NFS badge. The cap badge was worn with the dark blue and red-piped peaked cap worn when in uniform – but not attending an 'incident'. This cap often set AFS firemen apart from their regular brethren, who wore a peakless cap similar to the navy 'Nelson' cap. Typically, a double row of chrome buttons was a feature of the heavy wool fire tunic worn when attending fires, and when otherwise on duty.

Like all the Civil Defence services, the AFS was issued with the standard military issue steel helmet. The decision to provide these to the AFS, and later NFS, fire personnel was born of the need to effectively decontaminate helmets should the enemy use war gases. Cork and leather helmets would be less easily cleaned, and although the steel helmet presented a risk of electrocution when fighting fires, it was widely adopted. LFB helmets were distinguished by a broad red band, while AFS helmets were usually in factory-finish grey. London AFS helmets

London Auxiliary Firewoman driver Prunella Potts talks to a male colleague.
(IWM D 2616)

Left: The AFS tunic badge with area designation – in this case, London.

Below: The AFS cap badge.

The AFS silver buttonhole badge, awarded to early volunteers.

London Fire Brigade (LFB) steel helmet, distinguished by its red band.

Far right: London AFS steel helmet with its distinctive insignia.

London Auxiliary Fireman, with fire tunic, cap, webbing belt and pouch, and Service Respirator.

had their own distinctive shield badge. Senior officers (Divisional Officer and above) wore white helmets with red rank bands and the monogram 'AFS' in red; junior officers wore grey with white rank bands. Simple grey helmets were worn by Firemen; Leading Firemen had a narrow white band; Patrol Officers, two narrow bands, and Section Officers, one broad white band – earning these officers the name 'snowdrops'. In action, fire service steel helmets were used with a heavy oilskin hood, known as 'curtains'. These were part of the standard anti-gas kit, consisting of a reinforced band that fitted around the rim of the helmet, with a curtain of oilskin that draped down on to the fireman's shoulders, and fastening if required at the front. Although intended for gas protection, this hood also served to protect the wearer from water and sparks – and has helped define our image of the AFS man in action.

AFS firemen were dressed in normal uniform, with wool trousers, cap, and Service Respirator. This respirator was for use with 'war gases'; it was not proof against smoke or combustion fumes – specialist breathing apparatus would be needed for this purpose. The same wool tunics were used in action, the wool trousers covered by heavy two-piece oilskin leggings, the cap replaced with a steel helmet. Unlike regular firemen, AFS firemen were issued with only one, instead of the more normal two, wool tunics. This was to cause some resentment between regular and volunteer during the Blitz period, since AFS firemen were often called upon to attend the multiple incidents of the Blitz in wet tunics.

The standard personal equipment of all firemen of the period was a broad leather or webbing belt, to which were attached a hemp line (for a multitude of tasks, including lashing fire branches to ladders), a holder (known as a pouch) for the fire axe and, in London, one for a hose spanner. The fire axe itself was of two types; one was usually ash-handled, with a one-piece steel axe and pick, typical of firemen's personal equipment for decades. The other common fire-fighting axe issued to the AFS (and later the NFS) was the rubber-handled, steel-shafted 'Chillington Arpax', which was 'tested to 20,000 volts', in case of use against electrical cables. The possibility of electrocution was a serious threat to the safety of all civil defence workers, and as such this axe was widely distributed, used by the ARP Services as well.

Fire axes and webbing, part of the essential equipment carried by wartime firemen.

To house the AFS personnel, auxiliary fire stations were set up in a variety of buildings, dispersed throughout towns and cities to guard against being knocked out in one air raid, and were mostly issued with grey-painted trailer pumps – fire pumps to be towed behind any vehicle available, most commonly taxis in London. The AFS was put on war footing at the end of August 1939, with the call-up of the volunteers to full-time service, and with the issue of steel helmets and gas masks. From 1941 the AFS was to be swept up with the county fire brigades into the nationalised fire service, the NFS, and with it, the spirit of the volunteer.

AFS greetings card, 1940.

The men and women of the AFS were to be tested in the front line when the raids commenced in earnest in September 1940. The fire brigades were fractionated into small county brigades – estimated at around 1,400 in England and Wales alone, each with its own traditions, uniforms and equipment. This equipment would include hydrant types, hose connectors and branches. Brass fire hose fitments were, and still are, referred to as 'branches' in the fire service; they form the important 'business end' of the fire hose. Most brigades outside London used branches with an instantaneous fitting. In London, AFS firemen had not only to learn their trade with the standard equipment; they also had to contend with the additional complication of a screw fitting, which required the use of a hose spanner to ensure correct coupling.

A range of wartime fire branches; the two on the right use the instantaneous coupling system.

German 1 kg magnesium-bodied 'Electron' incendiary bomb, dated 1943.

These factors would cause issues for the fire services when there was a greater need to share manpower, experience and pumps. Each fire would be assessed by fire officers according to the number of pumps (fire engines) required to fight it. In normal peace time, a large fire would be 20 or so pumps; during the night Blitz in London, and in the dark days that followed, it was typical for 500–1,000 pumps to be required to fight one conflagration – fires raging out of control. Pumps from neighbouring forces would have to be drafted in. Early on, the Germans learned that although high explosives would wreak havoc on the infrastructure of Britain's towns and cities, to destroy greater areas required larger and larger tonnages that were beyond the capability of the twin-engined German bombers. Later, bombing tactics shifted to incendiaries, which were dropped in large clusters from within the bomber. Concentrated, these would be used to devastating effect against British city centres; later, this tactic would be used against the Germans themselves.

The standard German incendiary – the Electron – weighed 1 kg. It was composed of a central detonator and thermite (aluminium and iron oxide) charge that would set off the magnesium body, allowing the bomb to burn brightly, and with intense heat. On impact, the fuse engaged as the striker hit the igniting cap, setting the thermite alight; this burnt at around 2,500°C for thirty seconds, this in turn igniting the magnesium body. The bomb had to strike its target head-on to ignite, many bounced at an angle, failing to initiate. In most cases, the bomb would penetrate through normal roofing, with only concrete and earth being proof from its attentions. It burned with an intense bright white light – so intense that special goggles were issued to those dealing with these bombs – at about 1,300°C for around fifteen minutes. This would set fire to anything inflammable within a radius of a few feet, an extremely effective weapon, particularly when dropped in clusters from 'Molotov bread baskets'. Falling in a range of unlikely places, clusters of the Electron would soon burn out of control, and the fire services would then be hard-pressed to deal with the resulting conflagration. This would be a lesson hard learnt in 1941 with the largest incendiary bomb raids, particularly as a heavy Heinkel He 111 bomber could carry as many as 1,000 incendiaries at any one time.

At the outbreak of war, the AFS was called to a full-time wartime footing. The Phoney War was a trying time, but at least it meant that the AFS men and women could start to learn their trade. Drills were the order of the day, the firemen learning how to efficiently deploy their fire hoses, deal with ladder work and attempt rescue. As stated in the standard guide, *The Auxiliary Fireman* (1939), the primary role of the firefighter was the rescue of people at risk from fire before attempting to put out the blaze. Following that would be the chance to fight the fire using the taxi-towed trailer pump, capable of pumping some 350–500 gallons of water a minute. Knowing how to harness this modest power, and finding a source for its insatiable thirst for water, was a major duty of the fire service.

At a given station, the fire service would be divided into two watches – each with the station officer, sub-officer, duty-man, a pump crew (usually two or three men) and other crew members, with a duty officer. The watches were split between day and night. When a call was received from the ARP Control, or other means, the alarm would be sounded – 'the bells go down'. Crews would be deployed to the scene. In the early days of the Blitz, high

The Auxiliary Fireman and its successor, both authored by V. J. Wilmoth.

AFS firemen attacking a fire at Eastcheap, London, during the Blitz. (IWM HU 1129)

35

explosive bombs would accompany the incendiaries, and the lives of the firemen would be under threat from not just the fire, but also the smoke, the possibility of electrocution and the collapse of unstable buildings. AFS men had also to guard against the possibility of poison gases, much feared in the prelude to war. Rescue work was their prime consideration, and in this they would work with the other Civil Defence services. On arrival, the officer in charge would assess the situation; working together, the trailer pump crews would fight the fires. Water supply was a pressing need, and with the explosion of HE bombs, often hydrant pipes would be ruptured. Pipes would have to be set up to seek their cargoes from canals and rivers; later, bombed buildings would be used as tanks to house water, and permanent, street-level pipes laid. Fighting the flames, jets of water would be directed by men on the branches at the seat of the flames, and the fire attacked from all quarters until it was subdued. The men of the AFS would work through the night to attack their voracious enemy, consuming all in its path. Many would lose their lives in rescue work, crushed beneath falling buildings – famously depicted by AFS artist Leonard Rosoman, who witnessed colleagues crushed beneath a collapsing wall in Shoe Lane, London – and in battling the flames. Their woollen tunics would be wet through, their faces dirty from their grim battles – deserving of the Churchillian epithet 'heroes with grimy faces'.

A nightmare scenario; collapsing building in Queen Victoria Street, in the City of London, May 1941. A similar scene would be painted from first-hand knowledge by fireman-artist Leonard Rosoman. (IWM HU 650)

The 'three-quid-a-week army dodgers' would become the new heroes of the hour, and working with the regulars of the established forces they would become consummate professionals.

Fighting fires in wartime was hard. The life of the fireman was described by Commander Sir Aylmer Firebrace, in operational charge of the fire service: 'The fireman led a very hard, exhausting life during raiding periods. His fire kit, which included his gas mask, was heavy; long hours in fire boots made for acute discomfort; and often he was drenched to the skin. His worst sufferings were his eyes ... windstorms picked up sparks and brands and drove them into eyes, ears and skin. Thousands of firemen had to receive treatment at hospital ... a number, blinded.'

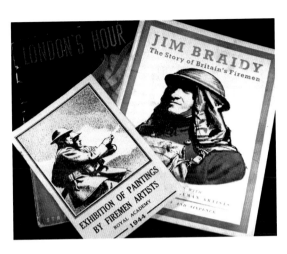

The outpourings of AFS artists.

As the war progressed, so it became apparent that the men and women of the AFS had other sides to their personalities; many were artists and writers. Their talents resulted in a new wave of artistic outpourings that would surface in such diverse places as the Royal Academy, to fund-raising publications and exhibitions for the National Fire Service Benevolent Fund, assisting the families of men severely wounded or lost in action. The AFS is well known for the number of gifted artists that joined its ranks. Their works would illustrate life in the dark days of 1940, and many now hang in museums and galleries as an evocation of the Blitz. They were also viewed during the war; the proceeds from admission being granted to the National Fire Service Benevolent Fund. *Jim Braidy*, written and illustrated by members of the NFS (most former members of the defunct AFS), tells the story of the fire service's equivalent of Tommy Atkins or Jack Tar. Illustrated by such notables as Paul Dessau, Stanley Froude and Leonard Rosoman, with literary contributions by William Sansom, James Gordon and Stephen Spender, this book is a reminder of the rich artistic legacy of wartime firemen. For many, the splendidly illustrated cartoon book *Heroes with Grimy Faces*, illustrated by Fireman Ben Betts, captures the spirit of the AFS volunteer in the early days of the war.

Heroes with Grimy Faces, cartoons of AFS life by fireman Ben Betts.

FIRE OVER LONDON

The Story of
The London Fire Servic[e]
1940-41
ONE SHILLING

THE NATIONAL FIRE SERVICE (NFS) AND FIRE GUARD

THE HARD LESSONS learnt from the Blitz period of 1940–1 demonstrated a need for a unified approach to fire fighting across Britain. The structure of the pre-war fire service owed much to its Victorian origins, and consisted of a large number of separate brigades, each with their own methods of working and equipment, each under the control of the local fire authority. In the provinces, this approach was reasonable, but in Greater London, the hub and junction of several counties, there were around sixty-seven individual brigades, with much potential for confusion and duplication of effort. It was agreed that, for London at least, these brigades would come under a single controlling authority in the event of war; this was later to form the model for the rest of the country.

The need for a single, unified fire service using the same regulations and, where possible, equipment, was born from the great fires of 1940, when London, Coventry and other cities were almost overwhelmed by the use of incendiaries. Although incendiaries were not previously considered a major threat, the 'Second Great Fire of London' in December 1940, and the intense raid of May 1941, both caused by incendiary attack, were to change this view. And so, in August 1941, the National Fire Service (NFS) was created, amalgamating the local brigade structure, and incorporating the volunteer AFS force on a full-time basis. The NFS was controlled centrally from the Home Office, but with considerable regional autonomy, and was divided across Great Britain into more than forty 'Fire Forces', each with its own Fire Force Commander, dispersed among the twelve Civil Defence regions. A fire force was composed of four divisions, with 200 pumps (and a further twenty in reserve). At its height, the NFS was to have 350,000 members – firemen and women – all of whom were to be actively engaged in the defence of the British Isles. Such a coordinated response was to ensure that 'Britain would not burn'.

Drill and training in new methods of fire fighting were an important part of the nationalised service, and a new Fire Service College was opened in Saltdean, near Brighton, in order to train fire officers and create excellence in the operational aspects of the Fire Service in war and peace. To cement the

Opposite:
Fire over London – the official story of the London Brigades' struggles in 1940–1. Lessons from the 'Second Great Fire of London' in 1941 led to the birth of the National Fire Service and the Fire Guard.

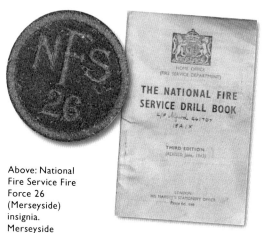

Above: National Fire Service Fire Force 26 (Merseyside) insignia. Merseyside received the second largest number of raids during the Blitz after London.

Above right: *The National Fire Service Drill Book*, 1943. The NFS was to be highly organised, and would be tested during the tip-and-run and Baedeker raids of 1942–3, the 'Little Blitz' of 1944 and the V-weapons offensives of 1944–5.

Right: *'In the Service of the Nation'. The NFS goes into Action*, a Raphael Tuck picture book from 1944. Illustrated and written by NFS personnel, proceeds from the book were to swell the coffers of the National Fire Service Benevolent Fund.

unity of the new service, as far as possible, the same uniforms, equipment and insignia were issued across the forty or so Fire Forces, the length and breadth of Britain. This was not always practically possible in terms of fire-fighting kit, but at least a means of marrying the previously mismatched equipment of neighbouring forces was found. Importantly, under a unified chain of command, men and women could be posted across the country and resources marshalled in those areas most under threat – something that would have been largely impossible in the old county brigade system. Thus, in the latter stages of the war, it was common for 'flying columns' of NFS men and women from the North to be deployed in the more hard-pressed southern ports, and in the capital itself.

Born of the experience of 1940–1, the NFS was not to receive the same baptism of fire that had been met by the men and women of the AFS, the London Fire Brigade (LFB) and its smaller colleagues during 1940–1. Highly coordinated and well prepared, by the time it was operational the NFS was ready to meet all that could be thrown at it by the enemy. Particularly important was tackling the supply of water, given the Blitz experience of HE bombs cracking water mains, thereby stopping the flow of water at critical moments. Boreholes were dug, steel surface pipes laid along gutters (more easily repaired), and emergency tanks made from the basements of bombed buildings and other similar suitable voids. Training included means of tapping into all water supplies to fight the flames.

With the major Blitz period over in late 1941 (with more to come), NFS personnel turned their hands to what was termed 'productive work on stations' during lulls between incidents: the manufacture of war materiel, the cultivation of foodstuffs and a myriad of other tasks. Engaged in the aftermath of the Baedeker raids on historic town centres in 1942, tip-and-run raids on the coastal towns, the combat of the deadly 'butterfly' anti-personnel bombs (which opened in flight, scattered and were found hung from rafters, trees and hedges), and during the 'Little Blitz' on London in early 1944, the NFS would nevertheless play an active part.

But in March 1944, the NFS would face its biggest challenge from the new and deadly threat of Hitler's revenge weapons – starting with the pilotless 'doodlebug', or V1. Anxious civilians in south-east England would hear the droning engine of these weapons, and listen anxiously for the engine note to falter and fail – presaging the coming explosion. The NFS would thus be fully committed in the last year of the

THE
NATIONAL FIRE SERVICE BENEVOLENT FUND.

SECRETS
OF THE
FLYING BOMB REVEALED

SPECIAL DETAILED SECTIONAL DRAWING
and
EXPLANATION OF HOW THE ROBOT'S
FLIGHT AND DIVE ARE AUTOMATICALLY
CONTROLLED

Reproduced by kind permission of
THE ILLUSTRATED LONDON NEWS

PRICE SIXPENCE

Reproducing a cutaway drawing of the V1 from the *Illustrated London News*, this leaflet was sold in aid of the National Fire Service Benevolent Fund.

NFS personnel in action at the site of a V1 flying bomb attack in Upper Norwood, South London, on 1 July 1944.
(IWM D 21248)

The NFS uniform and equipment drew from the experiences of the AFS and the county brigades. The example illustrated is from Bristol (Fire Force 17), and has a wool tunic (with plastic, economy buttons), heavy fire boots and leggings (more usually black oilcloth), and a steel helmet (with gas curtains). A Service Respirator is carried (although often discarded late war), as well as webbing belt, fire axe and hemp line.

Sussex NFS (Fire Force 32) fireman in uniform, c.1942.

war in combating the effects of this new and deadly form of warfare – ballistic missiles that would arrive without warning and strike deeply into the civilian heart of the capital city, and in the towns and fields of Kent, over which many passed, and some lingered. The NFS was to last until finally disbanded in 1948; by then 1,027 members of the fire services nationwide had lost their lives to enemy action, and more than 7,000 had been seriously injured.

Borrowing heavily from the now defunct AFS, all NFS insignia had at its centre the monogram 'NFS', similar in all respects to that previously used by the AFS. Replacing the AFS breast badge was a circular NFS badge, worn in the same position on the left breast. Bearing the monogram 'NFS' in a circle in red on blue, regional identity was supplied through the use of the fire force number. Early uniform issues to the NFS were reissued AFS tunics. This was a matter of expedient; on nationalisation, over a hundred thousand AFS tunics had been manufactured. As such, this and the AFS peaked cap were accepted as the standard uniform in the new service. Rank was indicated, as it had been in the AFS, by red stripes and 'pips' based on the design of the pump impeller; tunics with unadorned epaulettes belonged to an individual with the simple rank of Fireman. The fire tunic was worn with heavy oilskin leggings and boots, and the same heavy black-dyed webbing belt with chrome fittings used by the AFS. The uniform cap was the dark blue, red-piped, peaked version also adopted from the AFS.

In common with all Civil Defence services, the NFS used the steel helmet previously issued to the AFS, painted in olive khaki colour similar to that issued to the army. These steel helmets were distinguished by a red and brass coloured NFS cap badge transfer to the front, with the fire force number given in red on a white painted oval on the front brim. Rank was given by a range of colours and bands: lower ranks, as indicated here, wore the standard khaki colour helmet; high-ranking officers, commanding columns and above, wore 'aluminium-coloured' helmets. Leading Firemen commanded individual pumps; trailer pumps had a crew of four, with heavy units needing six. Additions of bands and increasing bandwidths indicated more senior ranks, two narrow red bands indicating Section Leader (commanding five pumps), a broad red band denoting Company Officer (commanding ten pumps). Similar ranks were recorded on women's helmets, but using white bands.

The NFS cap badge.

The 'Second Great Fire of London' on the night of 29–30 December 1940, when the Luftwaffe pounded the City with 100,000 separate incendiary bombs, alerted the authorities to the inadequacies of the system of fire control. Individually, the 1 kg 'Electron' magnesium incendiary bombs dropped during the Blitz and beyond could be controlled by sand or stirrup pump – as long as the fire could be reached in good time. It was intended originally that ARP wardens would tackle incendiaries, but with all the other duties that the ARP Services had to attend to, this was becoming increasingly

NFS steel helmets. The red band indicates that this helmet belonged to a Leading Fireman.

Unofficial Fire Watcher lapel badges. Fire Watchers were employed by all major firms in order to watch for incendiary bombs.

difficult. Wartime fires were exacerbated by the fact that by the time the fire services attended, it was too late, as the hot-burning magnesium of the 'Electron' incendiary had burnt its way through the roofs of helpless buildings. Up to 1941, wardens did not even have the right of entry granted to fire authorities, so British factories and domestic premises, often tightly locked, were left unprotected. To combat this, an unpaid force of Fire Watchers, armed with helmet and stirrup pump, were mobilised, and every industrial premises had an organised rota – although many resented the extra burden placed upon them after a hard day's work – with a minimum requirement to carry out 48 hours of duty in any four week period. These men and women were trained to locate and deal with incendiaries before they had taken hold of a building, before calling in the NFS.

In the streets, Supplementary Fire Parties recruited by the Fire Service, and Street Fire Parties (both SFP) recruited by the ARP, watched out over residential properties in the same way that the Fire Watchers did over industrial premises. In August 1941, alongside the founding of the NFS, the duties of the Fire Watchers and SFPs would be combined into one national organisation, the Fire Guard, under the control of local authorities, but trained to national standards. The Fire Guard grew in stature in 1942, when it was to be tested during the Baedeker Raids and 'Little Blitz', engaged in saving the historic structure of Britain's ancient towns and cities from destruction. Because of this, in 1943, the Fire Guard was completely separated from the Warden's Service to work closely with the NFS.

It underwent a dramatic expansion with compulsory service from those men and women not employed elsewhere – a move not universally popular. In the light of the mistakes of 1940–1, the Fire Guard was a highly organised service with large numbers of individuals not otherwise engaged on the Home Front enrolled in its ranks. Training in the techniques of tackling incendiaries dropped by 'Firebomb Fritz' was essential, and good instructors were in demand. By 1944, however, many of the duties of the Fire Guards had been superseded by events, as the war moved towards its conclusion.

Fire Watchers and Supplementary/Street Fire Party personnel were issued with a steel helmet, officially called the 'Civilian Protective Helmet', which had much in common visually with those worn by the medieval Yeomen of England. Possessing a high crown and a broad rim, the depth of the helmet and the orientation of its simple leather liner provided protection for the nape of the neck, as can be seen in the side view. The high dome of the helmet was also intended to allow indentation in the crown. Helmets of this type were mass produced; often they are marked with the letters SFP (Supplementary/Street Fire Party), painted directly on the light grey factory finish, or FG (Fire Guard), painted in black letters on a white painted helmet shell. Rank in the highly organised Fire Guard was indicated by one, two or three black hoops on the white helmet.

Official handbooks on fire prevention and fighting for the Fire Guard.

Civilian Protective Helmet as issued to Fire Watchers and the Fire Guard. The high dome was to allow for indentation. Cheaply produced, there are many still found today.

For most people engaged on fire watching duties, there was to be no uniform, but a simple arm band of Civil Defence dark blue was issued to indicate authority – first with the letters 'SFP' in red, then the words 'Fire Guard' in yellow (and, later on, white). In some cases, these armbands were adorned with white stripes to indicate rank. Worn with normal clothes, or in some cases, overalls, these armbands indicated to passers-by the duties of the wearer. They were granted to the bearer only after a course of instruction had been completed –

Above: Fire Guard armbands. The first pattern was gold on blue.

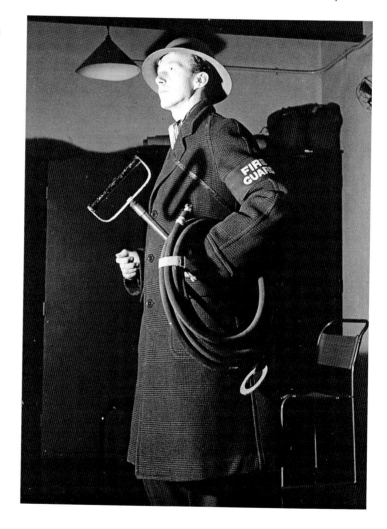

Staged British official photograph of a Fire Guard equipped with helmet and stirrup pump.
(IWM D 4984)

a badge of competency. Off-duty firewatchers, SFP and Fire Guard Personnel often took to wearing commercially produced lapel badges in a variety of bands to show their engagement in National Service.

By 1944, over six million people were registered for fire guard duties – men and women – though by this stage in the war there was notable absenteeism as the threats receded. In mobilising the country to all-out war, the Government recognised the need to prepare and train for a return to the firebomb campaign of 1941, when several of Britain's historic town centres were gutted for the want of coordinated action. This preparedness meant using what little time ordinary people had left in between work and home life. Under the *Defence (Fire Guard) Regulations* (1943), fire guards were expected to attend training in dealing with incendiaries. Failure to attend was an offence.

Wardens and fire guards would report the clatter of incendiaries raining down on the roofs of Britain at the height of the enemy raids. Later in the war, an explosive charge was added to the mix – this had a delayed action of one to two minutes, and was deliberately intended to kill or maim the civilian fire watchers and other members of the Civil Defence, and discourage them from guarding against the incendiary. Posters warned the public to be vigilant against the actions of 'Firebomb Fritz'.

Controlling a single bomb was well rehearsed, as it had been the subject of a series of Player's cigarette cards that showed all aspects of Air Raid Precautions, including the control of incendiaries with sand, scoops and stirrup pumps. Splashing with water would cause the bomb, burning at great heat, to explode into pieces that would scatter its fire everywhere. Outside of buildings, this would be an option, as it would accelerate the burn time from some twenty minutes down to seconds. A better option indoors was to spray the incendiary with a fine mist of water from a stirrup pump; this, too, would accelerate the life of the bomb to a quicker conclusion. Sand bags and sand scoops also provided means of containing the bomb's action, and of cutting down on the glare.

The stirrup pump was worked by a team of three people: one carrying out the pumping, the second directing the hose. Keeping the bucket adequately filled was the duty of the third member of the team. Stirrup pumps were issued to fire watchers and SFP personnel on the basis of one per three individuals. These pumps evolved from simple sprays with a foot

Stirrup pump, Redhill scoop, spade and incendiary bomb at the feet of a Fire Guard.

support used in gardening and whitewashing of outhouses. It was adapted from these mundane purposes by the experts of the Incendiary Bombs Committee, by the addition of a dual jet with a spray nozzle – the jet to tackle the fire, the spray being most effective against the incendiary bomb itself. In the words of the official historian: 'the stirrup pump must rank with the civilian gas mask as one of the chief protective instruments evolved for the use of British civilians in the Second World War.' Effective pumping speed when tackling incendiaries with the spray was thirty-five double strokes per minute, this delivered three-quarters of a gallon of water per minute in a spray radius of 12 to 15 feet. Such pumps would see much action in blitzed Britain.

The 'Redhill' container and scoop was a simple piece of technology of pre-war design that was intended to allow wardens and householders to protect their homes from incendiary bombs. The Redhill container was a squarish bucket with handle, intended to contain the incendiary bomb. Getting the bomb into the container was a tricky business, involving a harmless-looking scoop and hoe arrangement. Both

The operation of a stirrup pump against an incendiary bomb. Instruction provided by a pre-war cigarette card.

The operation of a Redhill scoop against an incendiary bomb. Instruction from a pre-war cigarette card.

scoop and hoe fastened together to give extra length where required. The intention, ably illustrated in the pre-war cigarette cards produced by the Imperial Tobacco Company, was that the hoe could be used to gather the incendiary into the scoop, which could then be placed in the sand bucket filled with sand. The sand would help contain the flames, and be readily removed. Unwieldy, this was to be superseded in effectiveness by the stirrup pump; but sand was maintained as an effective means of combating the incendiary, with sand bags for the purpose left at lampposts – often the target for dogs in need of relief. Other means of dealing with incendiary bombs included specially designed long-handled grabs, intended to dislodge incendiaries from inaccessible positions.

Together, the NFS and Fire Guard represented the best lessons learned from the Blitz of 1940–1; with the increase in random firebomb attack, they were always on hand to ensure that Britain would not burn. In London alone, some 327 men and women of the London fire services were killed, 3,000 injured, with 50,000 war emergency calls answered.

The Fire Services Memorial opposite St Paul's Cathedral, set up by Cyril Demarne MBE in memory of all the firefighters, men and women, who lost their lives in the war.

THE POLICE

THE POLICE, the traditional guardians of the peace, of law and order and the protectors of the public, would be at the centre of civil defence activities in wartime Britain. With Britain under air attack, they were expected to continue their peacetime duties, but with added responsibilities. It would be the police who first sounded the sirens before and after air raids; who evacuated areas threatened by unexploded bombs; who controlled and diverted traffic and people away from an incident, and in many cases took charge of the coordination of effort at a bomb site. In the provinces, police officers would also take charge of incidents on the ground, taking on the role of incident officer in London. Outside London, the chief police officer could also be the ARP controller. Through it all, the police would be in the thick of the action.

Few wartime photographs of bombing incidents do not have a 'bobby' in attendance, often steel-helmeted. Outside London, and acting as incident officers, police would coordinate the various Civil Defence services required to deal with an incident, logging the activities of each service, and maintaining an incident post. As the 'Operational Booklet' for Birmingham City Police (a city heavily bombed during the Blitz) put it: 'The duties of the incident officer will include the diversion and control of traffic ... the closing of roads, evacuation and barricading of areas as necessary, the posting of police officers and members of the wardens service ... By tact and persuasion the best use should be made of all personnel at the scene ...' Police officers were trained to recognise 'objects dropped from the sky' — usually bombs of some sort — and would be on hand to ensure that any unexploded bombs would be cordoned off, and the public held at bay in the interest of their own safety.

If there was one aspect above all others that dominates the whole war experience on the Home Front, it is that of the blackout. Universally disliked, it was introduced just before the outbreak of war, on 1 September 1939. The blackout was intended to reduce the target for enemy bombers, and was vigorously enforced, with householders and businesses both being under

Opposite:
A police constable
in wartime rig.
(IWM D 3977)

A 'bobby' at the scene of a personal tragedy. PC Frederick Godwin consoles a man from Upper Norwood who has just lost his wife and home to a VI flying bomb, 1944. (IWM D 21213)

scrutiny from the police. In the pre-Blitz, 'Phoney War' period this led to culprits being served with stiff fines, and in some cases imprisonment and drastic action – at least one policeman in London was killed while trying to scale a drainpipe to extinguish an upstairs light. The blackout was total in the early stages of the war. Cars, buses and the general public, not used to the night sky, were expected to navigate the streets safely in near pitch darkness. Many people were tragically killed in road accidents, with a doubling of casualties in the first few months of its introduction. By Christmas of the first year of war, shops and restaurants were once more able to show somewhat subdued lights; by the New Year, pinprick 'glimmer lighting' was provided on some streets. If Britain was to continue going about its business, then road traffic would have to operate; therefore, the lighting restrictions for military vehicles were applied to commercial and private vehicles. Car headlights were blacked out so that only a thin strip of light could be seen; later, specially designed hoods to Home Office specifications like the example illustrated – with diffusers and guards to prevent light spilling upwards – were to be attached to the headlights of commercial vehicles to guide them through the gloom. The police had strict and precise instructions, with light 'not exceeding 2.5 foot candles at 10 feet from the lamp', 'foot candles' equalling the light given by one candle at a distance of one foot. Restrictions were eased following the end of the intense Blitz, and as the war ground to a conclusion the blackout became a 'dim-out' in September 1944, with lighting levels similar to that of a moonlit night sky. A welcome return to illumination finally came on 30 April 1945, when Big Ben was lit symbolically once more.

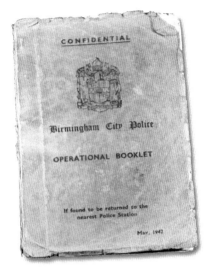

A wartime 'Operational Booklet' from Birmingham City Police. This indicated the duties of the police, from enforcing the blackout to identifying bomb types.

With invasion and the possibility of enemy paratroopers dropping from the sky, the still-unarmed police were to be vigilant. Enforcing Winston Churchill's 'Stand Firm' policy formed part of the operational aspect of the police, ensuring that the population did not make 'unwarranted movements'; that is, in the event of invasion, there would not be mass panic and migration. Identity cards, carried at all times, would be checked. Police were empowered to take control of traffic during invasion conditions, allowing only permitted vehicles (displaying ELs or 'Emergency Labels') and demobilising others. The spreading of 'false rumours' likely to induce panic, and the possibility of the open looting of food supplies were also to be police matters. Fortunately, these aspects of civil defence were not to be tested.

Ensuring the public were warned off from unexploded bomb (UXB) sites was part of a policeman's duty. Signs like this would be set up where necessary.

KEEP CLEAR UNEXPLODED BOMB

Blackout lamp 'hood' from wartime vehicle. Light was diffused by a screen in the body of the hood, while shields ensured that only thin strips would be seen at the front, projected down onto the road. Enforcing the blackout was a constant task for the police.

More commonly, the police were also on hand to take into custody downed airmen (often for their own safety) and, perhaps more controversially, to take charge of enemy aliens – people from the Axis powers living in Britain. Following the invasion of the Low Countries by the Germans in May 1940, and the fear of 'fifth column' activity, police officers were instructed by Churchill to take into custody all enemy aliens (Germans, Austrians and Italians) living in Britain (and registered with the police) who were deemed to represent a security risk. This risk had been assessed by special tribunals as categories 'A', high security risk; 'B', doubtful; and 'C', no risk (many of whom were refugees from Hitler's Germany). Of the first two categories, some 6,350 individuals were taken into custody, to be interned in barbed wire camps on the Isle of Man and elsewhere; very many more were left free. Most would be released as the invasion threat subsided.

Above: Special Constabulary insignia, including buttonhole badge, belonging to a 'Special' from Southampton.

Right: Special Constabulary medal issued for service in the Second World War. It was first instituted in the Great War for war duties.

Above: The young person's Police Auxiliary Messenger Service (PAMS) wore no uniform initially; instead, this lapel badge was issued to indicate a young person was 'on war work'.

Prior to the outbreak of war, there were fifty-eight county police forces and over twelve hundred borough and city forces in Britain – many of which were very small. As with the fire service, the raising of reserves and auxiliaries as a supplement to the regulars was seen as a very necessary component of the wartime Civil Defence services. As such, in wartime, there were to be three police reserves, two of which were already established. The First Police Reserve comprised retired officers, generally 'pensioners' over the age of 55, who had volunteered to serve again should the need arise. The Second Reserve was also a familiar one; the Special Constabulary, a force of unpaid civilian volunteers. A buttonhole badge to distinguish Special Constables who had undergone a period of training was approved by the Home Office in March 1939. Given the pivotal role that the police were expected to play in any future conflict, particularly in London, a third reserve was also needed, the Police War Reserve. Comprising male volunteers of 25–55, they, like the men and women of the Auxiliary Fire Service, were liable for call-up to full-time service in time of war. This reserve force was raised originally for the Metropolitan and City of London police forces in 1938, but was later extended to the whole country. Full-time women police officers were few; as such a women's auxiliary – the Women's Auxiliary Police Corps (WAPC) – was also raised for women aged between 18 and 55, as was a messenger service – the Police

Standard wartime blue cloth-covered, cork police service helmet for the Metropolitan Police with blackened 'night duty' helmet plate – introduced in wartime, and used until the early 1950s. More often than not this would be replaced by the steel helmet.

Police steel helmets. The steel helmet was worn together with the standard blue serge uniform and Service Respirator when raiders threatened. Special Constables and War Reserve Police Officers wore the steel helmet at all times; usually marked 'SC' or 'WR' to indicate the wearer's service. As with the regulars, rank was denoted by the addition of transfers bearing stripes and 'pips' as appropriate, in this case by a sergeant of the Special Constabulary.

In common with the fire services, the police were to carry the Service Respirator, as issued to the armed forces. This example belonged to Special Constable 142 E. J. Pickford serving in the coastal town of Bournemouth.

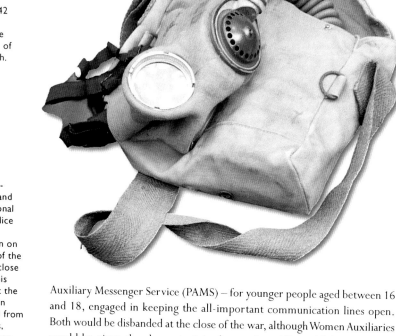

The blue-and-white duty band was a traditional symbol of police authority in London. Worn on the left arm of the police tunic, close to the cuff, this indicated that the wearer was on duty, as it had from the early days, when policemen were expected to wear their uniforms at all times.

Auxiliary Messenger Service (PAMS) – for younger people aged between 16 and 18, engaged in keeping the all-important communication lines open. Both would be disbanded at the close of the war, although Women Auxiliaries would be given the chance to join the regulars. All would do their bit in maintaining order on the streets in wartime.

The steel helmet was worn together with the standard blue serge uniform and Service Respirator when raiders threatened. In all other circumstances, a traditional blue cloth-covered, cork service helmet was worn with a blackened 'night duty' helmet plate – introduced in wartime, used until the early 1950s, and an enduring symbol of the British 'bobby' in peace and war. Special Constables and War Reserve Police Officers wore a steel helmet at all times, this being the usual headgear of the War Reserve. Otherwise indistinguishable from the standard steel police helmet (although commonly with the addition of white bands), membership of the reserves was usually indicated by the addition of letters 'SC' or 'WR' to indicate the wearer's service. In common with

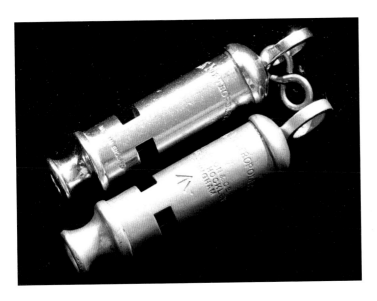

The General Service Whistle or 'Metropolitan' had replaced a variety of alarm rattles in the latter part of the nineteenth century. The 'Metropolitan' was designed to allow the whistle to be held by the lips alone while blowing it – an improvement on earlier tapered versions.

the fire services, the police were to carry the Service Respirator, as issued to the armed forces.

The blue-and-white duty band was a traditional symbol of police authority in London. Worn on the left arm of the police tunic, close to the cuff, this indicated that the wearer was on duty, as it had from the early days, when policemen were expected to wear their uniforms at all times. In the Blitz, this duty was to be an onerous one. Another traditional police accompaniment, the General Service Whistle or 'Metropolitan', had replaced a variety of alarm rattles in the latter part of the nineteenth century. The 'Metropolitan' was designed to allow the whistle to be held by the lips alone while blowing it – an improvement on earlier tapered versions. During wartime, other services carried similar Hudson whistles – sharp blasts from which were intended to sound the alarm in air raids and incendiary attacks – which led to the possibility of confusion.

A relatively new innovation at the time was the women constables of the Women's Auxiliary Police Corps. They were to wear a uniform, in London at least, that was similar in most respects to that of their army counterparts in the ATS. Belted, open at the collar, and worn with white shirt and black tie, the uniform was finished off with a cap identical in all but colour and badge to that of the ATS. Elsewhere, more unbecoming uniforms and headgear were issued by some authorities, often with an armband as the preferred insignia, bearing the letters 'WAPC'.

Women constables of the Women's Auxiliary Police Corps were to wear a uniform, in London at least, that was similar in most respects to that of their army counterparts in the ATS. Belted, open at the collar, and worn with white shirt and black tie, the WAPC tunic also bore light blue embroidered shoulder titles like the unissued example illustrated.

THE WOMEN'S VOLUNTARY SERVICE (WVS)

THE Women's Voluntary Service for Air Raid Precautions (later for Civil Defence) was established in 1938 under the charismatic leadership of the rather imperiously titled Dowager Marchioness of Reading – the widow of a former Viceroy of India. Lady Reading had had a long history of involvement in voluntary service through the Personal Service League, founded in 1932 to assist the unemployed, and was a positive role model for many women. She was to be the inspiration and foundation of the new service. The need for the Women's Voluntary Service (WVS) was born out of the recognition that in the coming conflict women would form an essential part of the Civil Defence services; yet despite this, few had come forward to join the developing ARP.

Something had to be done, and as such, the then Home Secretary, Samuel Hoare, asked Lady Reading directly to plan and develop a new service that would fully engage women in civil defence. The WVS as envisaged by its leader would be democratic, open to all comers and initially at least, devoid of uniform. At first, the intention was to stimulate the enrolment of women in the ARP Services, and to bring home to women the reality of air attack. Later, it would encompass much more than that. By the end of 1938, enrolment lay at just over 32,000 women. From this humble start the WVS was to take on more and more tasks on the home front, with a total enrolled membership of just over 960,000 women engaged in all tasks from billeting and welfare of evacuees and bombed-out people; direct involvement with the ARP Services; running rest centres and incident enquiry points; providing staffing for canteens and mobile catering units for workers, members of the armed forces, and air-raid victims; engagement in National Savings initiatives (collecting for the war savings weeks); and development of salvage drives.

Early in the conflict, the WVS was to have a major role in the support of the mass evacuation of children and the elderly from city centres. With the predicted danger that vast aerial armadas would obliterate cities, it made sense to remove the most vulnerable from harm's way. The women of the WVS were on hand to help, both with the loading of their vulnerable charges

Opposite:
Stoic member of the WVS Housewives Service, wearing her husband's medals from the Great War together with ARP, WVS and WI (Women's Institute) badges. The WVS would be a mainstay of Home Front effort. (IWM D4862)

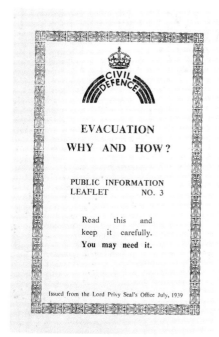

Above: Saving for the war effort was an important public service. The WVS was instrumental in assisting with War Savings Weeks.

Right: The evacuation of children and other vulnerable citizens from city centres in 1939 was a momentous and heart-rending task; the WVS was to be ever-present, assisting with the transport and billeting of anxious young people. This leaflet from 1938 outlines the evacuation policy.

onto trains, and in the billeting of children (and young mothers) at their final destination on the outbreak of war in September 1939. The WVS would justly receive accolades for their achievements.

Together with local authority employees, the WVS staffed rest centres. Rest centres provided temporary accommodation and food for the thousands made homeless during the Blitz.

Salvage Steward Badge. Salvage – recycling in today's language – was an important part of the war effort, and the WVS played its part.

When the bombing began in earnest in 1940, the WVS was on hand to help with the clothing and feeding of those made homeless. At major bombsites, WVS canteens served refreshment and succour to the men and women searching for survivors, shoring buildings, and fighting fires. For those made homeless, rest centres, set up as temporary respites for those bombed out of their homes, were staffed by the volunteer women of the WVS who worked alongside local authority personnel. Salvage drives – recovering valuable metals, paper, rags and bones, were also organised and held by the women of the WVS.

Many families lost everything in raids, and WVS members worked tirelessly to source clothing, running their own used clothing stores, and also to help distribute the 'bundles for Britain' directed from sympathetic United

States citizens. Later, WVS personnel served at Incident Enquiry Points (IEP), developed to support those who were seeking information about the aftermath of raids, the whereabouts of victims, and the ways of gaining victim support. The WVS Housewives Service comprised members unable to engage full-time in civil defence work due to their heavy domestic commitments. These women devoted what time was left to the support of vulnerable members of their own neighbourhoods, and in assisting the locally based ARP wardens in their many roles. There was room for everyone in the WVS.

With the diversity of members, roles and responsibilities in the WVS, it was felt that, like the ARP Services, the only distinguishing item should be a lapel badge, to be worn with civilian clothes. The resulting badge, designed by Marples and Beasley of Birmingham, was pin-backed, and consisted of a brightly polished 'white metal' rectangle surmounted by a crown, bearing the letters 'ARP' over the words 'Women's Voluntary Service', both picked out in red. This badge was issued from the inception of the service in 1938, but was thought to give undue prominence to the large 'ARP' letters, and as such, from February 1939, the lettering was changed to read 'WVS' with the words 'Civil Defence' below. This badge was worn on clothing, including everyday clothes, and from June 1939, the left lapel of the official coat issued to members. With the increased use of uniform, these simple insignia were to become cap badges on the felt hats commonly worn by the WVS. This felt hat – modelled on that worn by school girls – was chosen because it was hardwearing, and could be worn in a variety of shapes, but from 1941 it was replaced by a green beret, the WVS badge being attached to that.

The need for a uniform became apparent from the early days of the new service. Women volunteered from all walks of life, and varying means; the issue of a uniform would instil pride and reduce potential friction between members. Lady Reading was to invite designs from a number of leading designers; those of Digby Morton,

Above: The WVS Housewives Service played an active role in supporting the vulnerable members of local communities.

Left: The original WVS service badge, clearly indicating its role in ARP work.

Below: The second pattern badge, giving more emphasis to the WVS in its own right.

WVS cloth badges, worn with the specially designed uniform.

comprising coat, skirt and greatcoat, were chosen. Green was to be the dominant hue, but, given that there were superstitions about this colour, grey was woven into it, the composite colour achieved helping to hide dirt and dust. Unlike the other Civil Defence services (although in common with the Women's Land Army), members of the WVS were expected to buy their own uniforms – using valuable clothing coupons in so doing. The WVS coat was distinguished by a cloth badge, which was worn on the left lower sleeve.

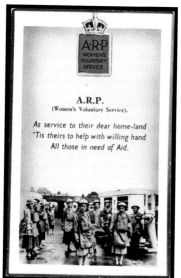

A.R.P.
(Women's Voluntary Service).

As service to their dear home-land
'Tis theirs to help with willing hand
All those in need of Aid.

An early war postcard celebrating the work of the Women's Voluntary Service for ARP.

The list of WVS involvement on the Home Front is seemingly endless, and the active engagement of women in these roles during the Second World War was to earn the service the title Women's Royal Voluntary Service, under which it continues to serve the wider community today.

FURTHER READING

Anon. *Front Line 1940–1941*. HMSO, 1942.

Billingham, Mrs A. *Civil Defence in War*. John Murray & The Pilot Press, 1941.

Brayley, M. J. *The British Home Front, 1939–45*. Osprey, 2005.

Brown, M. *Put That Light Out! Britain's Civil Defence Services at War 1939–1945*. Sutton, 1999.

Calder, A. *The People's War*. Jonathan Cape, 1969.

Doyle, P. & Evans, P. *The Home Front 1939–1945*. British Wartime Memorabilia. Crowood, 2008.

Gardiner, J. *Wartime Britain 1939–1945*. Headline, 2004.

Glover, C. W. *Civil Defence*. Chapman & Hall, 1938.

Marwick, A. *The Home Front*. Thames and Hudson, 1976.

Mills, J. *A People's Army. Civil Defence Insignia and Uniforms, 1939–1945*. Wardens Publishing, 1993.

Mills, J. *Doing their Bit, Home Front Lapel Badges 1939–1945*. Wardens Publishing, 1996.

Nixon, B. *Raiders Overhead*. Lindsay Drummond, 1943.

O'Brien, T. *Civil Defence*. HMSO & Longmans, Green & Co, 1955.

Priestley, J. B. *British Women Go to War*. Collins, n.d.

Spender, S. *Citizens in War – And After*. Harrap, 1945.

Strachey, J. *Post D, Some Experiences of an Air Raid Warden*. Victor Gollancz, 1941.

Web, E. & Duncan, J. *Blitz Over Britain*. Spellmount, 1990.

Wallington, N. *Firemen at War. The Work of London's Fire-fighters in the Second World War*. David & Charles, 1981.

Whiting, C. *Britain Under Fire. The Bombing of Britain's Cities, 1940–45*. Leo Cooper, 1999.

Ziegler, P. *London at War*. Sinclair Stevenson, 1995.

INDEX